ALL ABOUT
DYSPRAXIA

Understanding Developmental Coordination Disorder

KATHY HOOPMANN

Jessica Kingsley Publishers
London and Philadelphia

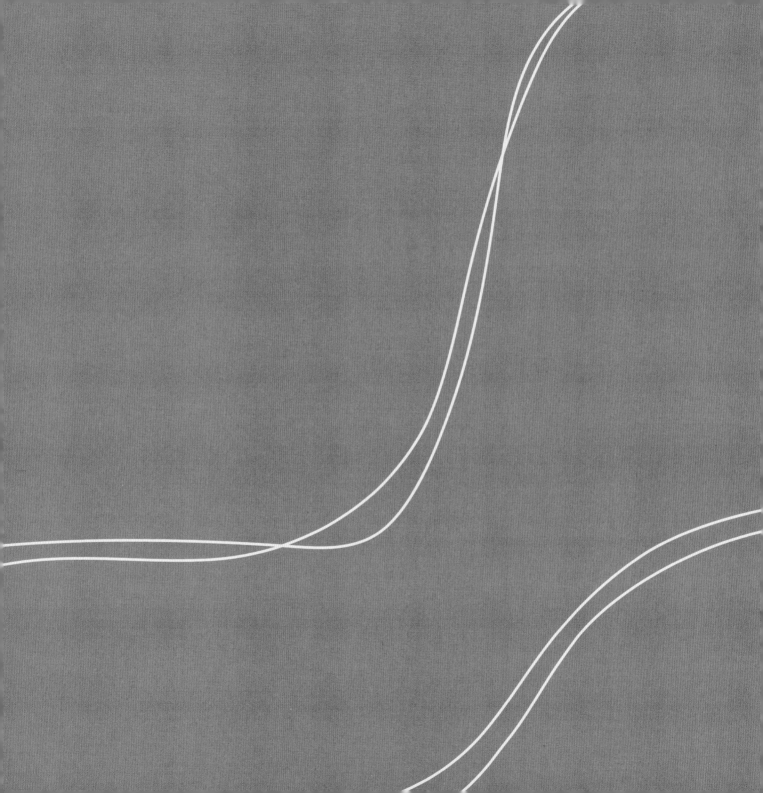

This book is dedicated to the dyspraxic community worldwide.
Thank you for sharing your stories with me.

A NOTE FROM THE AUTHOR

In the past, dyspraxia has been called Childhood Motor Deficiency Syndrome, Clumsy Child Syndrome and Perceptual Motor Dysfunction, among other terms. The word 'dyspraxia' does not appear in the DSM-5 (Diagnostic and Statistical Manual of Mental Disorders), where the condition is called Developmental Coordination Disorder (DCD). Dyspraxia is frequently co-morbid with other conditions such as autism, ADHD and dyslexia, to name just a few.

However, all this clinical talk cannot take away from the fact that with awareness and support from those around them, people with dyspraxia can learn and thrive. They have bright, inquisitive minds, are great at thinking outside the box, and often succeed in their chosen fields through determination and hard work and a good dose of humour.

To truly understand the strengths and challenges of dyspraxia and then to encapsulate its essence into a picture book, I needed a lot of help. Particular thanks go to the following people for their time, wisdom, insight, feedback, encouragement and editing skills: Judit Kiss, Alison Patrick, Kylie Cox and Carter, Warren Fried, Dr Kieran Flannigan, Kirsten Harpley, Samantha Fleming Elders and Kai, Helen Green, Gwen Liddle, Abigail Smith, Rhonda Valentine Dixon, Susie Griffiths, Rebecca Houkamau and last but not least to my husband, Errol Hoopmann.

Some people think dyspraxia is all about being clumsy, but there is much more to it.

1

Those with dyspraxia have brains that are wired differently from others. This can affect many parts of their lives, from how they move to how they think, learn and manage their day.

The first signs can appear quite early, with little ones being extra wobbly and late to walk.

The messages from their brains to their bodies are mixed up or delayed, which leads to all sorts of challenges.

They can trip over anything, even things that aren't there, and can feel unsteady just walking from one place to the next.

Getting dressed can be tricky,

and buttons and shoelaces are hard to master.

7

They often topple, spill or break things,

even though they try to be careful.

They are not sure what strength to apply so may
use too much pressure, or not enough.

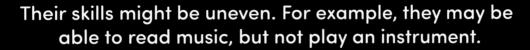

Their skills might be uneven. For example, they may be able to read music, but not play an instrument.

Learning to balance or ride can take a long time,

and sports can be challenging.

They can become good at avoiding activities
if they fear that they might fail,

and need understanding and encouragement to keep trying.

15

When activities are broken down into smaller parts, and they are given heaps of practice, they manage much better.

First, grab the rope. Then *swing*!

It helps when they are shown what to do.

Turn your head more.

When everything is overwhelming, a hug and being encouraged to *take a breath* and *relax* can work wonders,

then celebrating every success makes all the effort worthwhile.

Mixed messages from the brain can also cause low muscle tone so those with dyspraxia may do tasks more slowly than others.

Some have extra flexible joints that are easily stretched, which makes their body ache.

Even sitting uses loads of muscles, so they can't do that for long!

Besides, they listen better when they move.

Reading may be tiring as it's not easy to track each line.

Letters may blend together until one word blurs with the next.

and often their writing is messy and difficult to read.

They might prefer to type than write by hand.

When they can't keep up they may be called naughty or lazy,
despite working harder than everyone else to do the same job.

Every day
is exhausting,

and they need rest breaks to have the energy to go on.

Being given more time to grasp new ideas allows
them to show their hidden talents,

and if they are offered choices, they are
more likely to try something new.

If needed, help from experts can build up their skills and confidence.

Having opportunities to explore what they love best means that their life is not always focused on the things they can't do well.

35

Sometimes, those with dyspraxia have problems with the muscles in their mouths.

Swallowing and blowing may be difficult.

They may trip over their words

and eating might be awkward.

Being a messy eater is sort of cute when you are young, but not so charming as you get older.

Planning ahead for possible problems
can help prevent embarrassment.

When going
out for dinner, don't
order spaghetti.

41

Dyspraxia can also affect the way they learn. If too many
instructions are given at the same time, it's like being in a whirlwind
and much of the information flies past and is gone.

They may struggle to remember what they were supposed
to do, and when and how they were supposed to do it.

This can impact many areas of their lives, such as finding stuff, finishing tasks, paying attention and planning activities.

Explaining things may be hard.

And they can get lost even in familiar places.

However, lists
and timers
and diaries
and colour-coding
their schedules,
can help them
organise their days.

Having instructions repeated and being asked, "Would you like some help?" gives them a reason to keep trying.

Once they do learn something, their long-term memories can be incredible.

Even with support, there are times when some with dyspraxia believe that everyone else gets on with life while they are left behind.

Understanding others is not easy, and they feel
different from those around them.

They may avoid mixing in groups for fear that their difficulties will be exposed.

In turn, others sometimes have trouble understanding those
with dyspraxia, and are not sure how to include them.

If all their efforts to
keep up and behave
are ignored, and they
are told that they are

too clumsy,
not trying,
not listening,
just being lazy,

they may become
anxious or depressed,

and lose the motivation
to keep trying.

However, those with dyspraxia *are* very clever and they *do* work very hard and they *are* great company, but because they think and move differently, not everyone can see how amazing they are.

They brighten up lives with their wit and laughter.

Often, they have a great sense of empathy

and check to see that others are okay.

They are inquisitive and may be unconventional

and can solve problems in unique and interesting ways.

Some are
exceptionally
creative.

Those with dyspraxia have individual strengths and challenges, so their needs and wants will be different.

When they are understood, motivated and supported, they
can become *really* determined and through sheer persistence
are capable of succeeding at anything they want.

So even though dyspraxia remains with them all of their lives, with their clever minds, their strong work ethic and their inventive ways of adapting, their futures look bright.

Animal names and photograph credits

Cover
Giraffe © Sergey Nivens

page 1
Alpaca © Fuller
Photography

page 2
Dormouse (Muscardinus
avellanarius) © Angyalosi
Beata

page 3
Baby raccoon © Jay
Ondreicka

page 4
Dogs © alexei_tm

page 5
Emperor penguins © Mario_
Hoppmann

page 6
Nigerian dwarf goat
© PioneerMountain
Homestead

page 7
Gerbil © Camilo Torres

page 8
Black and white rat
© Grace800

page 9
Jack Russell dog © Lazy_
Bear

page 10
Lion cub © Stu Porter

page 11
Poodle © ThamKC

page 12
Flying squirrel © Ekachai
prasertkaew

page 13
Great Dane © Dmussman

page 14
Guinea pig © Olena
Kurashova

page 15
Baby elephant © John
Michael Vosloo

page 16
Orangutan © BARON ILYA

page 17
Meerkats © sebast90

page 18
Orangutan and baby
© michel arnault

page 19
Panda © V-yan

page 20
Snail © k-02

page 21
Orangutan © Konstantin
Tronin

page 22
Rabbit © Rita_Kochmarjova

page 23
Polar bear with cubs
© Belovodchenko Anton

page 24
African hedgehog
© Kuznetsov Alexey

page 25
Peacock © Curioso
Photography

page 26
Rooster © Milos Batinic
| Maths formulas
© ChristianChan

page 27
Australian goanna/lace
monitor (Varanus varius)
© Rowan S

page 28
Rabbit © Africa Studio

page 29
Mouse © Sergey Bezgodov

page 30
Squirrel © leedsn

page 31
Brown bear (Ursus arctos)
© Sergey Uryadnikov

page 32
Polar bear and cub
© Belovodchenko Anton

Disclaimer: Animal names were identified by the photographers where available and all mistakes are unintentional. All photographs courtesy of Shutterstock.co.uk

page 33
Orangutan © apple2499

page 34
Egrets © tahirsphotography

page 35
Harvest mouse © Alan Tunnicliffe

page 36
Chipmunk © colacat

page 37
Gorilla © David Carillet

page 38
Pied veiled chameleon © Kurit afshen

page 39
Ground squirrel © Miroslav Hlavko

page 40
Baby African spurred tortoise © seasoning_17

page 41
Raccoon © Landshark1

page 42
Ladybug © Sasha Chornyi

page 43
Mandrill © Rebius

page 44
Rabbit © Seregraff

page 45
Alpaca © Lainea

page 46
Baby raccoon © Heiko Kiera

page 47
Mouse © Alexander Sviridov

page 48
Adult emperor penguin with chick © Roger Clark ARPS

page 49
Tortoise © David Carillet

page 50
Various animals © Artem Avetisyan

page 51
Sheep © taviphoto

page 52
Rabbit © Rita_Kochmarjova

page 53
Domestic rabbits © Shcherbitskaya Anna

page 54
Crowned sifaka lemur (Propithecus coronatus) © Dawn Quadling

page 55
White bear © Kwadrat

page 56
Dolphin © Alberto Andrei Rosu

page 57
Grey seals (Halichoerus grypus) © Ian Dyball

page 58
Monkeys © Hung Chung Chih

page 59
Bay horse © Rita_ Kochmarjova

page 60
Newborn chicks © Gecko Studio

page 61
Squirrel © blewulis

page 62
Parrot © LILAWA.COM

page 63
Frogs © Arif Supriyadi

page 64
Rhino © gualtiero boffi

page 65
Lion cub © Ekaterina Brusnika

First published in Great Britain in 2022 by Jessica Kingsley Publishers
An Hachette Company

1

Copyright © Kathy Hoopmann 2022

All photographs courtesy of Shutterstock.co.uk

All rights reserved. No part of this publication may be reproduced,
stored in a retrieval system, or transmitted, in any form or by any
means without the prior written permission of the publisher, nor be
otherwise circulated in any form of binding or cover other than that in
which it is published and without a similar condition being imposed
on the subsequent purchaser.

A CIP catalogue record for this title is available from the British
Library and the Library of Congress

ISBN 978 1 78775 835 3
eISBN 978 1 78775 836 0

Printed and bound in China by Leo Paper Products

Jessica Kingsley Publishers' policy is to use papers that are natural,
renewable and recyclable products and made from wood grown
in sustainable forests. The logging and manufacturing processes
are expected to conform to the environmental regulations
of the country of origin.

Jessica Kingsley Publishers
Carmelite House
50 Victoria Embankment
London EC4Y 0DZ

www.jkp.com

in the same series

All Cats are on the Autism Spectrum
Kathy Hoopmann
ISBN 978 1 78775 471 3
eISBN 978 1 78775 472 0

All Dogs Have ADHD
Kathy Hoopmann
ISBN 978 1 78775 660 1
eISBN 978 1 78775 661 8

All Birds Have Anxiety
Kathy Hoopmann
ISBN 978 1 78592 182 7
eISBN 978 1 78450 454 0